there was a big

J fish...

There was a big fish in the sea,
That ate swimmers and small fish for tea.

LIMERICKS

by Janeen Brian & Gwen Pascoe
Illustrated by Steven Woolman

Produced by Martin International Pty Ltd
[A.C.N. 008 210 642] South Australia
Published in association with Era Publications,
220 Grange Road, Flinders Park, South Australia 5025

Text © Janeen Brian and Gwen Pascoe, 1992
"There was a big fish in the sea," © R. Martin, 1992
Illustrations © Steven Woolman, 1992
Printed in Hong Kong
First published 1992

National Library of Australia
Cataloguing-in-Publication Data
Brian, Janeen, 1948—   .
        There was a big fish . . . limericks.

        Includes index.
        ISBN 1 86374 037 6.
        ISBN 1 86374 019 8 (pbk.).

        1. Limericks, Juvenile. I. Pascoe, Gwen,
        1942—   . II. Woolman, Steven. III. Title.

A821.0750803

Available in:

Australia from Era Publications, 220 Grange Road, Flinders Park,
South Australia 5025

Canada from Vanwell Publishing Ltd, 1 Northrup Cresc., PO Box 2131,
Stn B, St. Catharines, ONT L2M 6P5

New Zealand from Wheelers Bookclub, PO Box 35-586, Browns Bay,
Auckland 10

Singapore, Malaysia & Brunei from Publishers Marketing Services Pte Ltd,
10-C Jalan Ampas, #07-01 Ho Seng Lee Flatted Warehouse, Singapore 1232

United Kingdom from Ragged Bears, Ragged Appleshaw, Andover,
Hampshire, SP11 9HX

United States of America from AUSTRALIAN PRESS ™,
c/- Ed-Tex, 15235 Brand Blvd., #A107, Mission Hills CA 91345

there was a big fish...

There was a big fish in the sea,
That ate swimmers and small fish for tea.
He grew quite tremendous,
But his end was horrendous.

LIMERICKS

by Janeen Brian & Gwen Pascoe
Illustrated by Steven Woolman
Edited by Rodney Martin

Introduction

A limerick is a nonsense verse in five lines, with an AABBA rhyming pattern. Limerick is also a town in Ireland. How a verse form came to be named after it is unclear. Possibly it arose from an old party game in which guests sang a nonsense verse and chorus containing the words 'Will you come up to Limerick?'

Limericks appeared in 1822 in a book called 'Anecdotes and Adventures of Fifteen Gentlemen'. The adventures of one character, the *Man of Tobago*, were written as limericks. But it was Edward Lear who made the limerick popular. Lear, born in 1812, was one of twenty one children. He became a book illustrator, but he also enjoyed playing with words. He drew illustrations to *The Man of Tobago* and wrote his own limericks. Lear combined the third and fourth lines into one, and often the final line was a repeat of the first, for example:

> There was an Old Man with a beard,
> Who said, "It is just as I feared! —
> Two Owls and a Hen, four Larks and a Wren,
> Have all built their nests in my beard!"

The limerick is still a popular form of nonsense verse. Its set style makes it simple to write, but creating *funny* verse is always a challenge.

Gwen Pascoe and Janeen Brian wrote this anthology of limericks around several themes, including names of people, places and occupations. Sometimes they simply focused on the clever use of words and sounds. Steven Woolman, the illustrator, has added his own sense of fun with the big fish hidden in each page spread. But remember as you laugh, that:

A bright young person like you,
Might think this looks easy to do!
Limerick writing
Is very inviting,
So why don't you try one or two?

GP

5

My Uncle declared, "To be slim,
One must go every day for a swim."
But a big fish for dinner,
Made Uncle much thinner,
And the bits that are left are quite grim!

JB

There once was a dentist called Laurel,
Who swam out to look at some coral.
To a shark alongside,
Laurel said, "Open wide!"
(Perhaps you can think of a moral?)

GP

With a ding and a dong on a bell,
Our pussycat fell in a well.
She swims like she's crawling,
Her breaststroke's appalling,
But her backstroke is looking quite swell!

JB

A frog in the class? What a lark!
Chuckled Tom, "That'll scare our Miss Park."
But he's not seen her since,
The frog changed to a prince,
And eloped with Miss Park after dark!

JB

Jack Horner was looking quite glum,
Saying, "Look at this fruit on my thumb."
He turned rather pallid,
And sighed, "It's fruit-salad!
I thought I had ordered a plum!"

JB

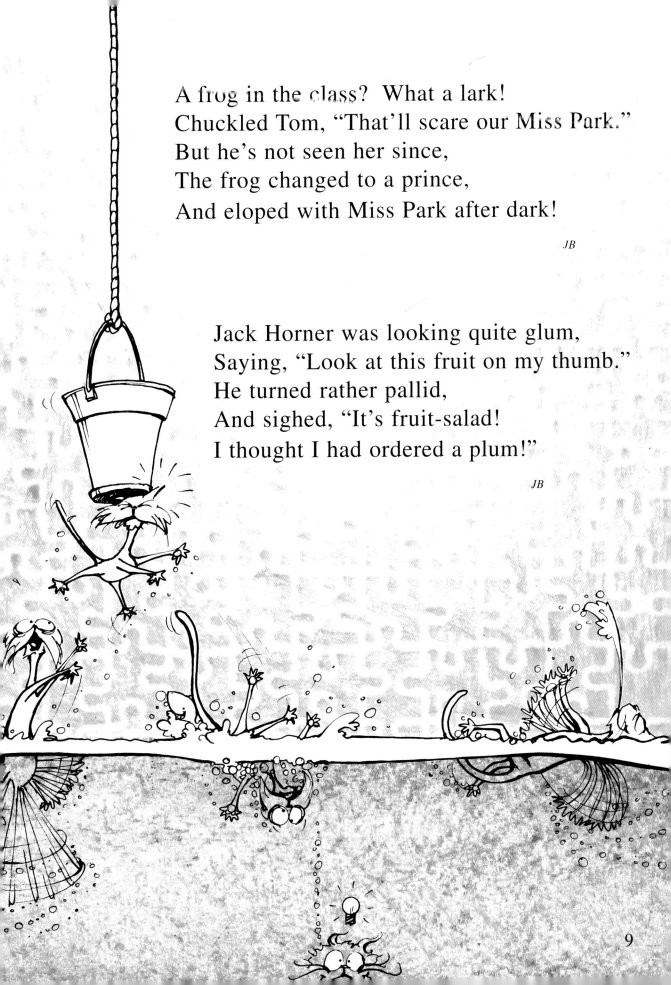

A ping pong player from Freeling,
Trod in dog poo and smelled unappealing.
His opponent cried, "Well!
I can't play with that smell,
You *pong* ev'ry time that you *ping*!"

A young girl was walking in Kent,
When she stepped on some fresh-laid cement.
To her shock and dismay,
It set straightaway,
And now she's a street ornament.

JB

Once an old man in Talbingo,
Jumped up and screamed out, "By jingo!
Some ferocious bull ants
Have crawled up my pants!
Bring something to help make the sting go!"

GP

A family who lived in New York,
Taught their pet parrot to talk.
Then the bird said , "O.K.
You can listen today,
It's my turn to teach *you* to squawk!"

GP

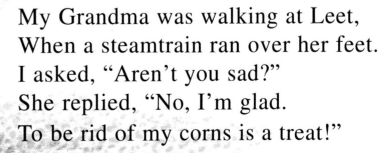

My Grandma was walking at Leet,
When a steamtrain ran over her feet.
I asked, "Aren't you sad?"
She replied, "No, I'm glad.
To be rid of my corns is a treat!"

JB

In a river in wild Kakadu,
Smiling crocodiles give you no clue,
Whether it's six or seven,
Or ten or eleven,
They're hoping to have lunch with you!

GP

"My tooth aches!" cried a crocodile from Billing,
So he went to the dentist for drilling.
As he opened up wide,
He felt hungry inside,
So he ate the poor dentist for filling.

JB

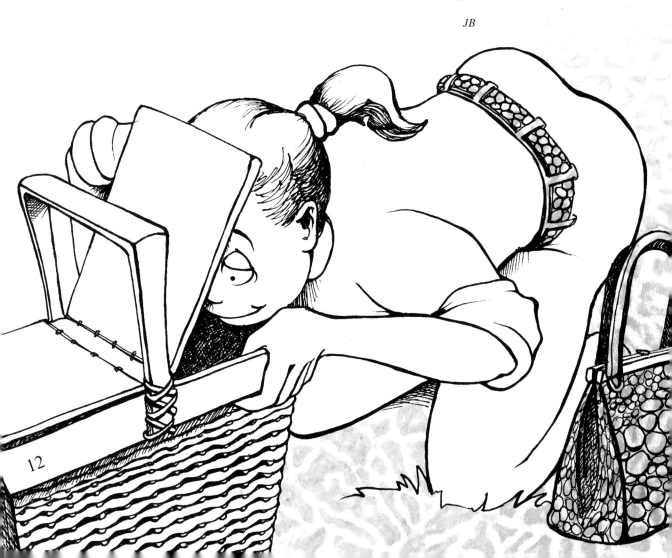

12

A television news commentator,
When pursued by a huge alligator,
Said, "It's time to take
A commercial break
For fast food . . . I'll be back later!"

When hiking, you must have the knack,
Of carrying loads on your back.
But when in Tibet,
Your very best bet,
Is to stack your back pack on a yak!

GP

Did you hear of the local town drama,
Involving a bull and a farmer?
One sat up a tree,
From ten until three,
Coming down when the other was calmer!

GP

This story is true (not a phoney).
I once rode a cow (not a pony).
She went very fast,
With her tail like a mast,
But her backbone was terribly bony!

GP

A flamenco guitarist called Lester,
Went to Spain for a music fiesta,
But Lester did play,
Nonstop, night *and* day,
Because Lester detests a siesta!

A problem occurred at our zoo,
When a baby was born to the gnu.
As they tried to announce it,
They couldn't pronounce it,
But of course the new gnu knew.

There was a young girl from Ipswich,
Who cried, "I've a terrible itch!"
The doctor just said,
"You're so horribly red,
I can't decide which itch is which."

JB

There once was an artist called Andrew,
Who laughed at anything Anne drew.
But he got a surprise,
When the judge gave a prize,
For the picture that Anne drew of Andrew.

GP

A butcher from old London Street,
Said, "Check ev'ry sausage you eat.
I don't want to alarm,
But most of my arm
Was, by accident, chopped with the meat."

JB

A seller of quick-setting plaster,
Said the plaster would help John work faster.
But this wasn't true,
For John slipped in the brew,
And now he's a plastered disaster.

GP

A clown tried to stifle a sneeze,
By giving his nose a tight squeeze,
But a bad cough instead,
Blew the wig off his head,
And his pants fell right down to his knees.

JB

There once was a girl named Rebecca,
Who captured and tamed a woodpecker.
She thought that its bill,
Would work like a drill,
And get her a job as a wrecker.

GP

An eager young cook one day,
Cooked in a most secret way,
A curry so hot,
It burned the pot
And melted the kitchen away.

GP

A dairymaid once in North Wales,
Went milking with two empty pails.
Milk — she got none,
But came home on the run,
For the *cows* in the field were all males!

JB

A remarkable lady from Crewe,
Cooked the vegetables that she grew.
But she slipped in her haste,
When she stooped for a taste,
And now she's the meat in the stew.

JB

There once was a chef from Dundee,
Who ate earthworms each night with his tea.
"The experts do say,
They keep illness away,
So that's why I do it," said he.

JB

There was a young pilot called Scoops,
Who enjoyed beef and vegetable soups.
But he cried from his seat,
"No more soup will I eat,
Before flying a loop-the-loop — *oo — oops*!"

JB

A snake to his girlfriend, Miss Gladys,
Said, "Nights are a bore for us adders."
And so in a thrice,
With a game-board and dice,
He said, "Let us play *Humans and Ladders*."

JB

There once was an athlete called Finn,
Who had grown so remarkably thin,
That when train doors shut SMACK!
He could squeeze through the crack,
Then get off the same way he got in!

JB

There once was a singer named Taurus,
Who worked with a pet brontosaurus.
If you opened your purse,
He'd sing you a verse,
And his pet used to join in the chorus!

GP

"Don't walk under ladders," said Fred.
"Or bad luck will fall on your head."
To avoid this event,
I stepped off the pavement,
And tripped on a black cat instead!

JB

There once lived a lady called Lisa,
Who was very well-known as a sneezer.
She sneezed with such power,
That she tilted a tower,
Her husband was building at Pisa.

GP

The people of John O'Groats,
Kept herds of shaggy old goats,
That ate flowers and weeds,
(Even packets of seeds),
And grew very flowery coats!

GP

There once was a goat from Dublin,
Who said, "I'm internally troublin'.
I swallowed some soap,
And now cannot cope,
For my insides are frothy and bubblin'!"

JB

At a flower show once in Australia,
A man showed a giant, red dahlia,
But it dropped so much pollen,
People's eyes became swollen,
So the judges declared it a failure.

JB

25

Did you hear about Peter from Weetah,
Who thought he could run like a cheetah?
He survived at the zoo
Just a minute or two,
For the cheetah was fleeter than Peter.

GP

There once was a worried young bear,
Who declared, "It is very unfair.
Whenever I cough,
Fur patches fall off,
And I fear that I'll soon be thread-bare!"

JB

On the floor of the Ark, there was mud.
Noah moaned, as he sat with a thud,
"If I hose it all down,
There'll be water around,
And the last thing we need is a flood!"

JB

A skunk in the zoo at Hong Kong,
Gave off such a powerful pong,
That visitors fled,
With faces quite red,
Crying, "Sorry, we can't stay for long!"

JB

The zookeeper said to the Llamas,
"I know you're a pair of real charmers,
But I really do mind,
When I come home to find
You wearing my best silk pyjamas!"

GP

A bootmaker called Mr Tweeky,
Had shoes which were horribly squeaky.
He picked up a gun,
And shot at each one.
Now his shoes are both squeaky and leaky.

JB

There is a young woman called Faye,
Who thinks about horses all day.
If she were able,
She'd live in a stable,
And instead of talking, she'd neigh!

GP

There was a young fellow called Hugh,
Who once spiked his hair up with glue,
But it set while he slept,
So he had to accept,
That his pillow went with his hairdo!

GP

The Roman Emperor Nero,
Wished to be known as a hero,
But you don't save a town,
By burning it down!
So Nero, as hero, got zero.

GP

A limerick writer named Gwen,
Who wrote this verse nine times, or ten,
Got such delight,
When it turned out right,
That she bit off the end of her pen!

Index of first lines

There was a big fish in the sea,
That ate swimmers and small fish for tea.
He grew quite tremendous,
But his end was horrendous . . .
'Twas another fish bigger than he (he! he!)

RM